Coasters of the 1970s (Volume 1)

by

Bernard McCall

In the mid-1970s, F T Everard embarked on a large newbuilding programme. This included four vessels of 1599grt but with a large deadweight of over 4000 tonnes. The order for three including two gearless went to Swan Hunter and the fourth, to be geared, went to Richards (Shipbuilders) Ltd at Lowestoft. This was the **Jack Wharton** which was built for Trent-based J Wharton (Shipping) Ltd but was bareboat chartered to Everard and always sported the Everard livery. She was launched on 18 August 1977 and completed on 28 October. She and her Tyne-built sistership took the Everard flag to areas never before visited. For example, **Jack Wharton** visited Yenbo in Saudi Arabia via the Suez Canal and Red Sea.

After the Falklands conflict, she also visited Ascension and Port Stanley. In early 1987 she was sold to Charles M Willie & Co (Shipping) Ltd and was renamed **Celtic Ambassador**. Sold to Greek owners in 1990 she was renamed **Smaro** and later changes of name saw her become **Riccam** (1993), **Ambassador I** (1996), **Clamba** (1998), **Captain Raffles** (2001), **Ferdinand** (2004) and finally **Regina G** (2007). Under the latter name, she traded in the Far East, generally between China, Korea and Russia. She was broken up at Jiangyin in China in May 2013. We see her passing Rozenburg on the New Waterway on 16 June 1984.

(David Gallichan)

INTRODUCTION

The 1970s proved to be a quite remarkable decade for coastal vessels. It saw so many changes that it is not easy to identify the most significant one. It was a time of general optimism within shipping and freight rates were relatively high for much of the decade. This resulted in a demand for new vessels and a more settled world meant that orders were being placed at yards as distant as the Far East and some orders made at European yards were being subcontracted.

Another important feature was the growth of container trades and the introduction of container feeder ships to serve these trades. Initially many of these feeders were multipurpose vessels able to handle general cargo in addition to containers but as the decade progressed there was a steady increase in the number of specialised feeders. As these appeared so was there a reduction in the number of coasters built with masts and derricks or cranes.

The final feature of the decade as far as the ships themselves were concerned was the appearance in its later years of specialised sea/river ships. There had long been coastal vessels designed for trading on the River Seine to Paris or River Rhine to Duisburg but the new generation had a hydraulic wheelhouse that could be raised and lowered according to the need to pass beneath low bridges.

There was one more important issue, though, and that was the change in manning regulations in the Netherlands in 1969. In the 1960s, competition from the Danish and German fleets had increased as they had used new tonnage rules to increase the size of vessels without breaking the paragraph limits. In 1969, the Dutch government introduced new rules based on the length of a ship, the new parameters being 60 metres and 75 metres between perpendiculars. Under these new rules, ships of up to 1599grt could trade under coastal manning regulations.

The main negative feature was the steady replacement of coal as domestic fuel by natural gas and this obviously had a considerable impact on the coastal movement of coal.

With so many changes taking place during the decade, I decided to publish the story in two volumes so that the many changes can be fully illustrated and discussed. In this volume, covering ships built in the UK, Ireland and Netherlands, we follow a geographical sequence of building yards. In the UK, we take a clockwise route from the Thames; in the Netherlands, we work from South to North.

Acknowledgements

It is simply impossible to name the very many people who have helped with this book. Some have answered a solitary question; others have provided a huge amount of information. I hope that all will accept these general words of thanks. I must, though, acknowledge the constant help and support of Gil Mayes and Bert Kruidhof. I readily thank the staff of Amadeus Press for their work. It would be equally difficult to acknowledge all the books to which I have referred. The publications of the World Ship Society, of Ships in Focus, and the marhisdata.nl website have been invaluable.

Bernard McCall   Portishead   November 2015

Published by Bernard McCall, 400 Nore Road, Portishead, Bristol, BS20 8EZ, England.
Website : www.coastalshipping.co.uk.   Telephone/fax : 01275 846178.   Email : bernard@coastalshipping.co.uk.
All distribution enquiries should be addressed to the publisher.

Printed by The Amadeus Press, Ezra House, 26 West Business Park, Cleckheaton, BD19 4TQ.
Telephone : 01274 863210.   Fax: 01274 863211.   Email: info@amadeuspress.co.uk;   Website : www.amadeuspress.co.uk.
ISBN : 978-1-902953-74-8

Front cover: The evening sunlight highlights the distinctive colour of the **Pavonis** as she cautiously navigates the River Ouse towards Goole with a full cargo of timber on 20 November 1977. Her hull was launched on 23 September 1976 at the Martenshoek yard of Firma Hijlkema & Zonen and she had the distinction of being this yard's final vessel. She was completed on 28 October by Scheepswerf "Voorwaarts" v/h E J Hijlkema, her owners being four members of the Groningen-based Salomons family plus Willem Oudman from Farmsum. Her first change of name was in 1992 when she was sold and renamed **Avoset**. On 29 April 1997 she left Moerdijk to cross the Atlantic to trade in central America. There was an odd occurrence in mid-July 1997 when she was reported to have been renamed **Nani**, a name change that lasted only two days. She did become **Nani**, however, on 12 September. Then owned in Colombia, she was renamed **Sos** in 2002, **Anancy** in 2003 and finally **Princess Aviv** in February 2006. During a fierce storm at Colon on 22 November 1996, she collided with another vessel and she is presumed to have been broken up nearby.

(David Gallichan)

Back cover: One of five vessels designed by Yorkshire Drydock for Bulk Cargo Handling Services, the **Seacombe Trader** was launched on 25 June 1974 and delivered three months later. She left Liverpool on 10 February 1989 and arrived in the River Thames in tow on 17 February. She was to have been renamed **Stone Trader** but seems never to have traded as such. In 1998 she was sold and renamed **Sibir**, becoming **Elf** in April 1999. She then worked in the Baltic mainly between Poland and Denmark. After grounding off Denmark in 2004 she was towed to Szczecin and was later slipped at Grimsby. In November 2004 she worked briefly in the Scottish timber trade but most significantly undertook a trial voyage along the Caledonian Canal to test the feasibility of the canal being used commercially. For this she was renamed **Calemax Enterprise** and by December she had returned to the Mersey to resume the work for which she had been built a quarter of a century earlier. She was laid up at Manchester in 2011 when the deliveries reverted to road transport. We see her in Irlam Locks on 1 February 2011.

(Bernard McCall)

Located at Greenwich, the shipyard of Cubow Ltd combined the building and repair facilities of W R Cunis and Bowker & King. The only coaster to be built at the yard in the 1970s was the ***Ordinence***, launched on 23 June 1978 and completed on 25 September for the London & Rochester Trading Co Ltd. On 5 February 1989 she arrived at Rotterdam from Invergordon and was sold to Onesimus Dorey (Shipowners) Ltd and bareboat chartered to Kirkwall-based Dennison Shipping Ltd by whom she was renamed ***Kava Sound***. When this company was in liquidation in spring 1994, the ship was repossessed and laid up at Birkenhead. She was soon sold to Scottish owners and renamed ***Nord Star***. As she passed through the hands of various Scottish owners over the next twelve years, she became a common sight in many of the small ports especially in western Scotland. Rather unusually, she was photographed as she left Aberdeen on 13 August 2004. In September 2009 she was sold to an owner in Togo and renamed ***Sea Gull*** under the Cameroon flag for trading along the coast of West Africa. Although thought to be still trading, no recent movements have been reported.

(David Dodds)

The shipbuilding and repair yard of J Bolson & Son was opened in Poole in 1922. It built a wide variety of vessels including minesweepers, passenger ships, dredgers and coasters. This vessel was ordered by the Hull Gates Shipping Company but the company was sold to Fred Parkes Shipping Ltd during construction and she was launched as *Parkesgate* on 22 November 1971 with completion on 27 January 1972. She was built for container routes linking Irish ports to Garston, Preston and Glasson Dock. In March 1979 she was purchased by Hay & Company, based at Lerwick, and was named *Shetland Trader*. She soon became a regular visitor to Sharpness delivering talc from the Shetland port of Baltasound, arguably the most northerly port in the UK. We see her arriving at Sharpness on 16 June 1996. Sold in 1997 she was renamed *Shetland Tramp* at King's Lynn on 17 May and after trading briefly in the Mediterranean she was resold and renamed *Arta* at Valletta on 4 November. Later changes of name saw her become *Marta* (1999), *Blameless* (2009), *Forthright* (2010), *Yinchuan* (2011). In December 2014 she became *Urios* under the flag of Tanzania.

(*Nigel Jones*)

Commodore Shipping had a well-established service linking Portsmouth to the Channel Islands. With the need to handle an increasing volume of containers, the company ordered the **Commodore Enterprise** from Appledore Shipbuilders. Launched on 28 October 1977 she was delivered in the following month and served the company for ten years. In addition to the Channel Islands service, she also made visits to the Iberian peninsula, notably Vigo and Lisbon, in addition to calls at Rotterdam and we see her in the New Waterway outward bound from Rotterdam on 10 April 1985. She arrived at Falmouth to lay up on 10 June 1987 but returned to Guernsey to destore on 18 August. Sold to Norwegian owners, she departed for Kopervik on the next day. Renamed **Scott Survivor**, by 1988 she was trading between New York, Miami and Port au Prince. In 1992 she was sold within Norway and traded mainly in the Caribbean but had moved to the Mediterranean by spring 1993 and then northern Europe by autumn. She arrived at Szczecin on 4 November and was renamed **Continental Alpha** on 3 February 1994, returning to service three weeks later. By the time that she was renamed **Victoria** on 1 April, she had returned to trade in the Caribbean. Acquired by the Wilson Group and renamed **Wilson Fjord** in 2002, she has since remained mainly in northern Europe.

(David Gallichan)

The **Leslie Gault** was launched by Appledore Shipbuilders on 3 June 1977 and delivered to Gallic Shipping in the following month. During the 1980s, like other vessels in the fleet (see page 61) she spent some time on charter to Kristian Jebsens Rederi and carried that company's funnel colours. Ownership passed to several companies but it was not until 1992 that she was renamed, becoming **Leszek G** under the flag of Poland. In 2000 she became **Jamal** following acquisition by owners based in Beirut and then **Maruf** after a sale within Lebanon in 2003. She reverted to **Jamal** in 2005 and was broken up as **Mr Goksu** at Izmir in early March 2011 having been renamed thus in 2007.

Her funnel colours show that she was on charter to Kristian Jebsen as she passed Meredyke on 25 May 1979. She was named after Jonathan James Leslie Gault, a director of Gallic Shipping. Shipbuilding at Appledore can be dated back to the mid-19th century, with Appledore Shipbuilders taking over from P K Harris & Sons in 1963. Since the 1980s, ownership of the yard has passed through various companies and at the time of writing it is owned by Babcock Marine.

(David Gallichan)

The town of Bideford on the River Torridge had a long tradition of boat building. Many vessels were built for the Admiralty at various yards. In 1964 a consortium of builders established Bideford Shipyard Co Ltd with a new covered construction yard. Fishing vessels, tugs and passenger craft were built here as was the coaster *Peroto*. The yard's closure in 1981 marked the end of shipbuilding in Bideford. She was launched on 15 November 1978 and completed on 15 March 1979. She was built for Cornish Shipping Ltd and regularly loaded china clay at Charlestown. A change of managers saw her renamed *Vendome* in 1994. She was arrested at Plymouth in April 1995 and was offered for sale by Lloyd's Bank. Bought by the Ramsey Steamship Co Ltd, she was renamed *Ben Maye*. She soon faced a problem. Having suffered an engine blackout when leaving Drogheda on 14 June 1995, she contacted another vessel and ran aground. She was refloated the same day with tug assistance and returned to Drogheda where repairs were carried out following the contamination of lubricating oil. In July 1997 she suffered major crankshaft problems. Sadly the Ramsey Steamship company was forced to close in 2014, having just celebrated its centenary. Its two remaining coasters were acquired by Kent-based Absolute Shipping and the *Ben Maye*, seen at Ramsey on 27 June 1995, continues to give excellent service.

(John Wiltshire)

The shipyard of Charles Hill & Sons was established in Bristol in 1845. It closed in 1977 although boatbuilding on a much smaller scale has continued on part of the site. Named after Miranda Guinness, Countess of Iveagh, wife of Benjamin Guinness, third Earl of Iveagh and Chairman of the Guinness company from 1962 until 1986, the **Miranda Guinness** had several claims to fame. Most notably she was the last ship to be built at the Charles Hill shipyard where she was launched on 9 July 1976. She was the world's first specially-built bulk beer carrier. Able to carry almost two million pints of Guinness in fifteen stainless steel tanks, she made her maiden voyage from Dublin to Runcorn on 26 January 1977 and was intended to make that voyage twice weekly. In 1993 she was sold following a decision to use transportable tanks for Guinness exports. She was renamed **Maigue** but remained in Bramley Moore Dock at Liverpool and was broken up there in early 1994. We see her in the River Mersey on 16 July 1979.

(David Gallichan)

The River Mersey is also the setting for the **Avondyke** on 29 August 1979. She was launched at the shipyard of Charles Hill & Sons on 27 August 1975 and delivered in January of the following year as **Skirbeck** to the Klondyke Shipping Company, based in Hull. This company's ships were named after Humberside locations that ended in _dyke so she was an exception. This was resolved in 1978 when she was renamed **Avondyke**, thus recalling the location of her builder whose yard had closed by then. Ownership later passed to North British Shipping Ltd. In late 1985 she was sold and renamed **Baronet** whilst retaining British registry. On 12 November 1985 she left Goole and sailed via Oristano, Suez and Aden to New Mangalore where she anchored on 19 December. She then continued trading mainly around the Indian sub-continent and was laid up at Mumbai (Bombay) after arrival on 11 August 1987. By spring 1988 she had been sold to Chowgule Steamships and renamed **Maratha Challenger** but she remained at anchor off Mumbai. She then disappeared from movement reports and eventually was reported to have sunk approximately 100 miles south of Mumbai on 16 July 1995.

(David Gallichan)

There were already several shipyards in Pembroke Dock when P Hancock moved there from Milford Haven soon after World War 1. The yard concentrated on the construction of fishing smacks and during World War 2 small vessels were built for the Admiralty. In the mid-1970s, the yard received an order for two coasters from R & H Hall, a Cork-based supplier of animal feeds, along with two sisterships for Coal Distributors Ltd. The first of the four was Hall's **Daunt Rock**, launched on 27 July 1976 and completed on 28 September. The yard closed after completion of the fourth vessel in the order in April 1979. Sold and renamed **Cornet** in 1988, the **Daunt Rock** remained in northern Europe for a further thirteen years. On 20 October 2000 she left the Danish port of Aarhus for Copenhagen and five months later she was reported to have been sold and renamed **Zila**. By late June 2001 she was reported at Jacmel in Haiti and then began to trade in central America. She soon disappeared from movement reports and in 2012 was removed from registers as her continued existence was in doubt. We see her approaching the entrance to the Manchester Ship Canal at Eastham on 3 September 1977.

(David Gallichan)

The **Vectis Falcon** was one of four ships, all fitted with four 12-ton derricks, ordered by Jebsens (UK) Ltd from the Ferguson shipyard at Port Glasgow in the mid-1970s. She was launched on 5 September 1977 and completed as **Clarknes** on 20 January 1978. After only five years in service she was sold to a Swiss company and was renamed **Fribourg**. A decade later she entered the fleet of Carisbrooke Shipping and was renamed **Vectis Falcon**. In 1998 her original 12-cylinder Allen engine of 2700bhp was replaced by an 8-cylinder engine of 1986bhp made by the Anglo-Belgian Corporation in Ghent. Following a sale to Greek owners in 2003 she became **Christos** under the flag of Georgia. In late 2004 she was acquired by Ukrainian owners and renamed **Anna**. She was broken up at Bassens in France in mid-2011. She was photographed at Newport on 25 August 1996.

(Nigel Jones)

Sistership of the **Vectis Falcon**, the **Georgios XII** was the second of the four vessels ordered from the Ferguson shipyard by Jebsen (UK) Ltd. Before construction began, the yard was taken over by the newly-formed British Shipbuilders and the order for this vessel was transferred to Scotts Shipbuilding Company at Greenock. She was launched on 30 September 1977 and was completed as **Clydenes** on 29 December. In 1982, she followed the **Clarknes** to Swiss ownership and was renamed **Sarine**. A sale to Greece in 1992 saw her become **Georgios XII** under the flag of Cyprus. A subsequent sale within Greece in 2003 saw her renamed, rather oddly, to **Georgios X. II**. In April 2005, she moved to Turkish ownership as **Vildirim K** and as such she was broken up at Aliaga in June 2012. The other two vessels in the four-ship order were not started as they were cancelled along with several other newbuildings for Jebsen as the company sought a more secure financial position. We see her outward bound from Fowey to Alexandria on 30 July 1999.

(Richard McCart)

Shipyards on the River Clyde were still flourishing when the **Westondyke** was launched at the Bowling shipyard of Scott & Sons on 5 October 1970. Shipbuilding at Bowling began in the early 19th century when the McGill brothers established a yard at the Forth and Clyde Canal basin. By the late 1840s the McGills joined with James Scott to form Scott & McGill, which became Scott and Sons in 1851. Between 1851 and 1979 Scott's built in excess of 450 vessels. In 1965, the company was taken over by Scott's Shipbuilding & Engineering Co Ltd, of Greenock. It later became part of the Scott Lithgow Group following the 1970 merger of Scott's Shipbuilding & Engineering Co Ltd and Lithgows Ltd, Port Glasgow. The yard closed in 1979.

The **Westondyke**, the first of two coasters built for Klondyke Shipping, of Hull, was launched on 5 October 1970 and completed on 19 January 1971. In spring 1982 she was sold to Cornish Shipping, of Plymouth, and was renamed **Cladyke**, her sistership **Fendyke** becoming **Clafen**. Sold in the following year, she remained busy in the clay trade from West Country ports as **Carmen** and under the management of Sanders Stevens. She arrived at Fowey on 17 July 1992 and was laid up. She left Fowey for Rotterdam on 1 May 1993, flying the flag of Honduras and named **Miriam**. She became **Miriam I** in 1998, **Le Cap Vert** in 1999 and **Mohamed Mustafa** in 2002. With existence in doubt, she was removed from registers in 2012.

(David Gallichan)

Although the 1970s may have started with optimism, that had largely dissipated by the end of the decade and many shipyards faced an uncertain future. In 1968 the Henry Robb shipyard at Leith merged with the Caledon Shipbuilding & Engineering Company in Dundee to form Robb Caledon Shipbuilders Ltd. The company became part of the nationalised British Shipbuilders in 1977 and closed in 1981. In the late 1970s, the company received an order for two vessels from Norwegian owner Paal Wilson and we include both. The *Salmo* was launched at the Dundee yard of Robb Caledon Shipbuilders Ltd on 17 August 1978 and was completed on 7 May 1979. She remained in the ownership of the Wilson Group throughout her career and arrived at Aliaga for recycling in late April 2014. We see her outward bound at Great Yarmouth on 22 March 2008 after discharging a cargo of stone.

(Ashley Hunn)

The two vessels ordered from Robb Caledon had been intended for the Hancock shipyard at Pembroke Dock but that yard had closed. In fact, the order was not for complete ships but rather for two hulls, with fitting out to be done in Norway. An innovation was that the ship's lines had already been generated by computer by her owners. The hull of the *Rhino* was launched at the Leith yard on 10 April 1978 and then towed to Norway for completion by Eides Sonner at Hoylandsbygd. In 1983 she was lengthened by ten metres.

Ten years later she was sold to Boa Shipping and renamed *Boa Rhino*. She reverted to *Rhino* when sold in 2007 since when she has had a variety of owners and flown the flags of several different nations. At the time of writing, she is owned in Piraeus and flies the Greek flag; her original 10-ton gantry crane has been replaced by excavator and grab. The Leith shipyard closed in 1983. She was photographed inward bound in the River Trent in 1981.

(David Gallichan)

The Everard fleet saw considerable expansion in the 1970s. This included eight dry cargo ships of 1599grt built at three different yards. The first pair were built by Richard Dunston at Hessle and differed slightly from the final six (see page 27). Four of the latter were constructed at Goole but the **Suavity** was the first of a pair from the Clelands yard at Wallsend. She was launched on 9 October 1972 and completed on 6 November. Like most of this group, she was sold in the mid-1980s. She was bought by Norwegian owners in 1984 and was renamed **Speedbulk**. Later changes of name saw her become **Corona** (1986) and **Birona** (1988) and then **Barco** in1988 when managed by Paal Wilson. She left northern Europe in early 2002 and began to trade in the Mediterranean as **Sea Trader**. We see her thus named in Limassol roads on 22 May 2003. She continued to trade in the Mediterranean area after becoming **Libya Star** in 2005 and **Twin Star** in 2008. She arrived at Aliaga for recycling in mid-July 2010.

(Nigel Jones)

Prince Line (1895) Ltd was established in 1895, bringing together a group of fourteen single-ship companies established by James Knott. Three years later, the company became simply Prince Line Ltd. It was taken over by Furness Withy in 1916 and it ceased to exist as a British shipping company in 1980 after C Y Tung bought Furness Withy. The **Chiltern Prince** was launched at Clelands' yard on 8 December 1969 and handed over to Prince Line in June 1970. She was one of four sisterships, three being built at Wallsend and the other by Grangemouth Dockyard. Prince Lines vessels were regular visitors to the Manchester Ship Canal and we see the **Chiltern Prince** at Eastham on 16 July 1980. Sold to the Government of Vietnam in mid-1981, she was handed over at Glasgow on 26 June and renamed **Friendship** under the flag of Panama. She passed south through the Suez Canal on passage to the Far East on 27 September 1981. Remaining in Vietnamese ownership, she was renamed **Thang Loi 02** in 1986 and was sold for breaking up in mid-2005.

(David Gallichan)

The second of a pair of ships built by Clelands Shipbuilding Co Ltd for the London & Rochester Trading Co Ltd, the **Luminence** was launched on 21 December 1976 and completed on 25 March 1977. She was one of several vessels in this company's fleet to have been converted for cable laying. Whilst most of these duties were local around the UK, the **Luminence** undertook cable work in Indonesia and in late 1982 sailed out to New Zealand to work in the Cook Strait. On this occasion she suffered engine problems and in November 1983 her original 16-cylinder British Polar engine was replaced by a 12-cylinder model from the same builder. In early 1999 she was sold to owners in Madeira and left Garston for that island on 18 March 1999. She then entered service between Lisbon and Leixoes. On 31 August 2002 she left Lisbon and four days later was renamed **Dream** by new Egyptian owners who traded her mainly in the eastern Mediterranean and Black Sea. Staying in Egyptian ownership, she was renamed **Green Cedar** in 2009 and is still in service in late 2015. We see her in New Zealand waters in March 1983.

(Bernard McCall collection)

Stephenson Clarke Ltd was one of the oldest shipping companies in Britain and from 1872 the company usually named its ships after towns and villages in Sussex and Hampshire. In 1928 Powell Duffryn acquired the entire share capital of Stephenson Clarke. In the 1970s the company ordered three coastal vessels, often identified as mini-bulkers, from Clelands. The first of these was the **Birling** which was launched at Wallsend on 31 August 1977 and delivered in December of that year. In 1995 she saw service transhipping coal from Hunterston to Kilroot. We see her approaching Bevans Jetty at Northfleet to load cement clinker for Leith on 29 July 1999. Sold in late summer 2000, she was renamed **Sofiakaterina** on 28 September and left Ipswich on 3 October,

bound for Palma (Majorca) and a new trading life in the western Mediterranean. In early January 2003 she was sold and renamed **Josephine I** but it should be noted that this was rendered as **Josephina I** in movement reports for the next two years. A sale and renaming to **Goodwish** on 21 April 2005 saw her trading in the eastern Mediterranean and Black Sea. She became **Vahhab** after a final sale in February 2008 and she returned to trading in the western Mediterranean. She arrived for recycling at Aliaga in late January 2010.

(Kevin Bassett)

The fifth vessel to have carried the name *Royal Prince*, this example was launched at the Swan Hunter shipyard on Tyneside on 17 October 1978 and completed in September 1979. We see her outward bound in the River Mersey on 10 January 1981. A charter to Ellerman as *City of Oporto* in 1984 was very shortlived. By early 1985 she had briefly reverted to *Royal Prince* and was immediately sold to owners in Thailand. She left Belfast on 12 February 1985 and passed through the Suez Canal on 24 February with Bangkok as her destination. Renamed *Thai Jade* under the Liberian flag, she commenced trading mainly between Bangkok, Kaohsiung and Hong Kong. She continued this trading pattern between 1985 and 1989 when chartered by Overseas Orient Container Line as *OOCL Ambition*. Renamed *Host Country* in autumn 1993, she was by then trading between Hong Kong and Shanghai. Later changes of identity saw her become *Jin Zhan* (1996), *Xiang Shan* (1998), *Yong He* (2001), *Onto Star* (2003), *Le Yu Quan* (2004) and finally *Quan* (2007). She arrived for breaking up at Chittagong in late March 2007.

(David Gallichan)

We now move to Humberside. The shipbuilding company Cook, Welton and Gemmell was established in Hull in 1883 and moved to Beverley in 1901/02. The company was taken over by C D Holmes in 1963 and a decade later it became part of the Drypool Group whereupon its name changed to Beverley Shipbuilding and Engineering Co Ltd. The yard was taken over by Whitby Shipyard in 1976. The only coaster built between 1973 and 1976 was the **Silloth Stag**, seen at Eastham on 24 July 1980. Ordered by Tilstone Construction, she was launched as **Tilstone Maid** on 31 December 1973.

Although completed on 25 March 1974, Tilstone did not take delivery and the ship was sold to North Shields-based Stag Line by whom she was renamed **Silloth Stag**. In 1985 she entered the fleet of Rix Shipping as **Robrix** and remained with the company for a decade, eventually becoming **Sprite** in 1995 and then **Konvik** (1997), **Edarte** (1998) and **Frojdi 1** (2002). Owned in the Albanian port of Durres since 1998, she is thought to be still in service although there have been no movement reports since 2013.

(David Gallichan)

The **Polarlight**, arriving at Goole on 7 August 1976, was one of four small identical coasters ordered by Eggar, Forrester (Holdings) Ltd. Two were built in Malta, one by Clelands, and this example by J R Hepworth at Paull near Hull. Long established as a broker, Eggar, Forrester was new to ship owning but had been attracted by grants and subsidies offered by the British government to buyers of new ships from British yards. All four were examples of the XL400 design (see page 32). She was launched on 10 March 1970 and completed as **Wiggs** on 17 April. In the mid-1970s, all four came under the control of Glenlight Shipping Ltd which, at about the same time, was taken over by the Clyde Shipping Company. The **Wiggs** was renamed **Polarlight** and it was hoped that she and her sisterships would be kept busy carrying bulk cargoes to the various sites in western Scotland where new rigs were under construction for the oil and gas fields in the North Sea. On 28 February 1989, she sank off the Isle of Man when heading for Ramsey with a cargo of cement from Magheramorne, near Larne.

(David Gallichan)

The *Locator*, photographed at Maldon on 9 September 1990, was the second of a pair of sisterships built for the London & Rochester Trading Co Ltd (Crescent Shipping) at the yard of J R Hepworth. She was completed on 3 September 1970. Both vessels are sometimes referred to as barges but this word seems to suggest trading only on inland waterways. The *Locator* and sistership *Lodella* both undertook voyages across the English Channel with the *Locator* especially regularly visiting Cherbourg with explosives. Both vessels were sold out of the London & Rochester fleet in August 1984 with the *Locator* being acquired by Bartlett Creek Shipping Ltd, owned by Alan and Annette Pratt. Seven years later, the *Lodella* joined her sistership in that fleet and the pair were supposedly bought by an owner in Galway in 2007. The *Lodella*, however, remained at Rochester.

(Bernard McCall collection)

The **Irwell Trader**, photographed on the Manchester Ship Canal, was one of five similar vessels built in the mid-1970s to transport grain, mainly maize, from Liverpool docks along the Canal to the premises of the Corn Products Co Ltd, later Cerestar, at Trafford Park. They were operated by Bulk Cargo Handling Services, a division of the Alexandra Towing Company and they remained in service until the late 1980s. The **Irwell Trader** was the last of the five to enter service. She and three sisterships were built by Yorkshire Drydock Company at its rather cramped yard on the River Hull. She was sold in December 1988 and was renamed **Tidal Trader**. She seems never to have traded as such and was laid up at Otterham Quay in March 1990. In June 1991 she and a sistership were sold to Portuguese owners for river trading and they were towed away from Gravesend on 26 July 1991. The rather box-like design of these five ships was deemed to be a considerable success and formed the basis of what was to be known as the "Yorkshire Coaster" design. Although sometimes considered to be barges, these vessels were all involved in coastal work later in their careers and so should certainly be considered to be coasters.

(Bernard McCall)

Having enjoyed the first experience of ship owning with the XL400 coasters (see page 22), Eggar, Forrester Ltd decided to invest in the "Yorkshire Coasters" series and we see two acquisitions at Brightlingsea on 15 July 1985. Both had arrived from Colchester ten days previously and were awaiting orders. The **Wis** was launched on 25 August 1976 and completed in January 1977 whilst sistership **Wib** was launched on 16 October 1978 with completion on 5 February 1979. They followed similar careers, both being purchased by Breydon Marine Ltd in mid-1986 and being renamed respectively **Breydon Venture** and **Breydon Enterprise**. In 1995 both entered the fleet of Rix Shipping Ltd and were converted to tankers. The former **Wis** became **Rix Hawk** and her fleetmate was renamed **Rix Harrier**. By 2014, both had been sold to Nigerian operators. The **Rix Hawk** became **Restorer II** but there is no new name for the **Rix Harrier**.

(Michael Warrick)

The Goole Shipbuilding & Repairing Company built nine ships for F T Everard during the 1970s. These included a group of four of which the **Fred Everard** was the first. All were built without cargo handling gear. She was launched on 15 May 1972 and completed on 7 July. She represented the company at the Jubilee Fleet Review at Spithead on 28 June 1977. She and her sisterships proved to be ideal multipurpose vessels, able to handle bulk cargoes in addition to timber, steel and containers. Sold to Maltese flag operators in mid-1985 she was renamed **Tara Bulk** and became **Mira Bulk** after purchase by Norwegian owners in 1987. Renamed **Mina** in 1996, she was broken up at Aliaga in 2010. With characteristic rust-streaked hull, she was photographed approaching Eastham Locks in the Manchester Ship Canal on 26 May 1978.

(Laurie Schofield)

A series of eight gearless coasters was built for F T Everard at three different shipyards with the first two coming from the yard of Richard Dunston at Hessle. Launched on 25 February 1971, the **Security** was completed on 27 April. All eight were built with the help of investment grants and the **Security** was the first Everard ship to use finance from outside the company. In 1986 she was sold to Carisbrooke Shipping and was initially renamed **Mark** but this soon changed to **Mark C**. She became **Elizabeth C** on 14 January 1996 and we see her as such at Sharpness on 7 July 1996. She arrived in Rotterdam in late October 1999 and was sold, departing one month later as **Eliza**. This was amended to **Elizabeth** on 27 April 2000. She arrived at Piraeus on 28 September 2000 and was renamed **Phoenix** six weeks later. She became **Agemar** on 6 November 2002 and moved from the Mediterranean to the Arabian Gulf. She disappeared from movement reports after arriving in Dubai from Somalia on 24 January 2004. She is understood to have been renamed **Sea Lion 1** later that year. She was removed from registers in September 2011 as her continued existence was in doubt. Dunstons bought the Henry Scarr shipyard in 1932 and went on to pioneer the use of all-welded construction in the UK. The yard eventually closed in 1994.

(Cedric Catt)

In the 1970s, apart from fishing vessels, the output of the Goole shipyard was dominated by vessels for the fleet of F T Everard. The **Martindyke** was one of only two exceptions. Launched on 2 December 1974, she was completed on 23 March 1975 for delivery to the Hull-based Klondyke Shipping. Most of these Goole-built vessels were intended for the timber trade from the Baltic and it was just such a cargo that the **Martindyke** was carrying when photographed arriving at Cardiff on 21 July 1979. She was sold in 1988, her new managers

being Torbulk Ltd based across the Humber in Grimsby. Then renamed **Rutland** this was amended to **Ruta** after a further sale in 1995. She arrived at Hull from Immingham on 7 November 1998 and was laid up awaiting sale. In spring 1999 she was sold to owners based in Miami and crossed the Atlantic to trade initially between Pensacola, Florida, and Cap Haitien in Haiti. She soon disappeared from movement reports and there is no further information about her.

(John Wiltshire)

The Goole Shipbuilding and Repairing Company moved to a site on the River Ouse in Old Goole in 1917. Exactly fifty years later it became part of the Swan Hunter Group's Small Ships Division and was nationalised in 1978. The yard closed in 1984 but was then bought by Cochrane Shipbuilders, of nearby Selby, with final closure coming in 1988. The **Authenticity** was launched on 12 July 1979 and completed on 23 October. She retained her name following a sale to Latvian owners in spring 2005. She arrived at Hull on 21 May 2008 and was handed over there, departing for Riga on 8 June. The next sale, in late 2007, saw her switch to the flag of Panama as **Caribe Trader**. She passed through the English Channel on 18 December 2007 and was noted at Miami on 4 January 2008 and at Mamonal, Colombia, four days later. She has remained in that area and regularly transits the Panama Canal. She is thought to be trading as a bunkering tanker.

(David Gallichan)

Sistership of the **Silloth Stag**, the **Maltese Venture** was launched as **Nellie M** at the Selby yard of Cochrane & Sons Ltd on 2 February 1972 and completed for Metcalf Motor Coasters during April. She was lengthened by eleven metres in 1978. On 7 February 1981, she was the victim of a bomb attack by the Provisional IRA when anchored in Lough Foyle. Refloated five days later, she was towed to Londonderry where her cargo of coal was discharged and she was eventually repaired. Renamed **Ellie** in 1982, she came into the ownership of Rix Shipping in 1984 and was renamed **Timrix**.

She became **Maltese Venture** in 1995 and we see her about to leave Cardiff on 14 June 1996. Renamed **Spezi** on 14 November 1996 she was sold in early 1997 to buyers in Colombia. After arriving at Ipswich on 17 March 1997, she spent a month under arrest and then departed for Antwerp. From there she sailed via Las Palmas to Colombia. She later became **Dove** (1998), **Amazon's Dolphin** (2003), **Oceanic Lady** (2009) and **Carmen II** (2011). She continues to trade in central America.

(Nigel Jones)

Photographed in the River Mersey on 19 July 1977, the **Saint Brandan** was the fourth vessel in the fleet of J & A Gardner to carry this name and was the second such multi-purpose vessel built for the company at the Wivenhoe shipyard of James W Cook & Co Ltd on the River Colne. She was fitted with a bow ramp able to take a wheeled load of up to 175 tons and could take 360 tons evenly distributed on her hatch covers. She remained on the slipway at her launch ceremony and a second attempt was also unsuccessful. It was some three weeks later, on 26 September 1976, that she eventually slid into the water. Despite this, she was handed over to her Glasgow-based owners on 8 December 1976, three weeks ahead of schedule. In May 1988 she was taken on long-term time charter by the Ministry of Defence for service in the Falkland Islands. In July 2009 she was bought by owners in Chile and transferred to the flag of that country without change of name. She has subsequently been modified with the removal of her bow ramp and the fitting of extra equipment.

(David Gallichan)

Shipbuilding had started on the site of the Cook yard in the mid-19th century. During World War 2, the yard was taken over by Vosper Ltd and built motor torpedo boats. It was bought in March 1947 by James W Cook & Co Ltd, Thames-based wharfingers and lightermen, and lasted until April 1986 when the company went into voluntary liquidation. On page 22 we refer to the XL400 design. This had evolved from the *Lady Serena*, built in 1964 for Rochester-based Thomas Watson (Shipping) Ltd by Clelands. The *Lady Sandra*, delivered from the Wivenhoe yard to the Rochester company in November 1970, was a near sister to vessels of the XL400 class. Sold within the UK in 1980 but remaining under Watson management, she was renamed *Labrica* as seen here at Meredyke on 11 August 1981. In 1983 she was bought by Dutch owners and renamed *Junior*. On 14 September 1987 her cargo shifted when she was about twelve miles off the Hook of Holland on passage from Rotterdam to Gunness. Abandoned by her crew, she was taken in tow on the next day but soon sank. On 27 September the vessel was raised and taken to Europoort for discharge. Not worthy of repair, she was delivered for breaking up at Hendrik Ido Ambacht.

(David Gallichan)

We now look at four vessels built in the Republic of Ireland. Rushbrooke Dockyard was established in 1853. Irish Shipping, the fledgling national shipping company set up a repair yard in Rushbrooke, and in 1957 they invited Dutch shipping magnate Cornelius Verolme to purchase the dockyard and assist in the development of the Irish shipbuilding industry. A total of 33 ships were built in what was known as Verolme Cork Dockyard which had over 1500 employees at its peak. Not surprisingly Arklow Shipping ordered several of its newbuildings from the yard, The Tyrrell family was one of the leading shipowners based in Arklow and a driving force behind the establishment of Arklow Shipping. The *Valzell* was launched at the Verolme Cork yard on 16 March 1976 and delivered to James Tyrrell Ltd on 1 June. We see her on the New Waterway on 15 August 1991. She left the Arklow fleet in 1996 following sale to Estonian operators by whom she was renamed *Skylark*. She retained that name after sale to Turkish owners in 2006 and was still trading in 2015.

(John Wiltshire)

The first of the Arklow coasters from the Cork yard in the 1970s was the *Darell* which was launched on 7 July 1970 and completed on 1 November. It has been suggested that she was intended to trade from Ringsend Dock in Dublin but it was found during construction that she would have been 15 metres too long to enter this dock's lock and so a section of that size was removed from her. She was renamed *Carrigrennan* after a sale to other Irish owners in 1974. She was approaching Eastham when photographed on 10 August 1981. In 1986 she was bought by Alderney Shipping. After a grounding in February 1989 she was sold to a captain in Canada and renamed *Free Trade*, becoming *Mother Wood* in 1994. She retained this name but transferred to the Panamanian flag after sale to an owner in Haiti in 2000.

The dockyard closed as Ireland's ship building industry collapsed in the early 1980s. Many of the yard's engineering and drydock facilities still remain and in 1995 it was acquired by the Doyle Group and has been operated by the Group's subsidiary Burke Shipping.

(David Gallichan)

The **Wicklow** was launched at the Verolme Cork dockyard on 26 June 1971 and completed on 6 October but was not commissioned until October 1972. For most of her career, she traded between Rotterdam, Antwerp and Dublin with Cork included for part of that time and Le Havre included latterly. In spring 1994 she was sold and, renamed **Wilke** on 31 March, traded between Antwerp and Riga. As **Wilke** she left Europoort on 18 December 1994 and sailed via Le Havre and Antwerp to Istanbul and Ashdod then on to Sri Lanka. On 1 May 1995 she was sold again and renamed **Vince**. She then traded between Hong Kong and mainland China. Later changes of name saw her become **Prince No. 5** in 2001, **Tian Mu** in 2002, and finally **Tian Feng** in 2004. She arrived at Jungjiang for recycling in late October 2011. She was photographed on the New Waterway on 1 October 1983.

(David Gallichan)

This vessel was the second of two sisterships built at the Cork shipyard for the British Railways Board. She was launched on 6 May 1970 and delivered as *Rhodri Mawr* in December. She was named after Rhodri Mawr who became king of Gwynedd in about 844BC. The ship was built to serve Dublin and Belfast from Holyhead but before she entered service a disastrous fire resulted in the closure of the Menai railway bridge, thus isolating Holyhead. Consequently the ships entered service linking Heysham to Belfast and the first sailing from Holyhead was on 31 January 1972. In 1973 she transferred to Harwich and took over the Parkeston Quay - Dunkirk service from *Brathay Fisher* as reported on the next page. With ro/ro traffic steadily superceding

containers on the Irish Sea, she had the dubious distinction of taking the final Holyhead - Dublin/Belfast sailing on 21 December 1989. In the following year, she and her sistership were sold to Piraeus-based Sarlis Container Services for whom she traded in the Mediterranean as *Peliner*. At the time, she began to carry two tiers of containers on deck; this was never done during her service on the Irish Sea. Sarlis suffered bankruptcy in 2004 and she was sold and renamed *Destiny*. A further sale saw her become *Yamm* in 2010 and she arrived at Aliaga for recycling in mid-November 2014. We see her passing through the Bosphorus on 9 August 2009 on a regular service linking Constanta in Romania to various Turkish ports.

(David Dixon)

We now look at ships built in Dutch shipyards. A shipyard at Deest was founded by Van Ooijen, Geurts and Van Gelder in 1870 and initially only wooden ships were built but steel vessels were later constructed at the yard. Around 1920 the brothers Hendrik and Otto van der Werf arrived from Groningen and developed the shipyard to become an important employer in the Deest region. The **Brathay Fisher** was launched at the van der Werf yard on 26 March 1971 and was delivered to Barrow-based James Fisher & Sons on 8 July. In August 1974 she was chartered for two years by British Rail and commenced work on the Harwich - Dunkirk route that had been opened in 1969 by SNCF. She was displaced from this route by the **Rhodri Mawr** on 23 December 1975 and in the following year was chartered by MacAndrews

and renamed **Calderon**. We see her at Eastham on 11 August 1978. Later that year she was again chartered by British Rail and reverted to **Brathay Fisher**. She worked on the routes linking Harwich to Dunkirk and Zeebrugge from 12 November 1978 to November 1980. She worked briefly between Dublin and Holyhead before being laid up for sale at Barrow. She left this port on 11 April 1981 after sale to Mediterranean operators as **Haje Naime**. Later changes of name saw her become **Violette** (1983), **Haje Naime** (1984), **Newpoint** and then **Pel Carrier** (1985), **Pancon 3** (1994) and finally **Progress 3** (2002). She arrived for breaking up at Chittagong in late June 2003.

(Laurie Schofield)

36

In 1974 the van der Werf shipyard was faced with financial problems and was taken over by the Bodewes yard at Millingen The difficulties continued and closure was announced in August 1975, with 240 staff and 60 subcontractors losing their jobs. The Bodewes yard itself closed in 2013. The ship seen here must come into the category of "mystery ship". She was launched at the van der Werf yard on 6 February 1970 and, although originally ordered by Gerhard Schepers, she was handed over to Italian owners as **Relay** on 24 April. The owning company was based in Genoa. A sale to owners based in Trapani in 1982 saw her renamed **Guido Baldo**. Throughout this time, she did not

appear in movement reports and this absence continued after she was sold and renamed **Atlantic Freighter** in 1993 and again after becoming **Sea Star X** in 1995. Sold once more in 1998, she was renamed **Margarita I** by a company called Margarita Cargo Line, based in Panama. She continued to be omitted from movement reports although a different vessel named **Margarita I** did appear in June 1997. She is reported to be still in service but there is no evidence of any port state control inspections. We see her at Havana on 23 March 1999.

(Nigel Jones)

We now turn to ships built at yards on waterways east of Rotterdam. The Lekkerkerk shipyard of T van Duijvendendik dated back to the 17th century. Arie Duijvendijk sold the yard in 1963 and it closed in 1975. The **Dalgo** saw many changes during her career. Launched on 23 May 1971, she was delivered as **Sassaby** to J Wiegman Shipping on 16 July. She was chartered to European Unit Routes, a subsidiary of P&O, for a container service between Tilbury and Rotterdam. This service later operated under the name of Containerlink. In 1983 she was sold and renamed **Saby** by Norwegian owners. She arrived at Gdynia on 2 July 1990, departed for Ålesund on 8 August and

was there converted to a self-discharging bulk carrier. She resumed trade as **Dalgo** on 18 October. We see her in the Elbe estuary on 7 August 1995. She left Bruges on 11 April 2001 and passed Cape Finisterre heading south three days later. The next report finds her in Beirut in February 2002 and by June of that year she seems to have been trading as **Houda** although this is not recorded in registers. The next recorded name change is **Houda F** and she was reported thus at Limassol in mid-February 2003. In 2006 she became **Azeza Moon** and continues to trade in the eastern Mediterranean, mainly to ports in North Africa.

(Bernard McCall)

In 1909, de Groot & van Vliet took over the Schram shipyard at Slikkerveer. It remained independent until a merger with IJsselwerf in 1977. A decade later all building ceased at Slikkerveer. This vessel was launched at the Slikkerveer shipyard on 26 November 1971 and delivered to Waling van Geest as **Geeststrom** on 17 February 1972. Her owners had a hugely successful trade out of Maassluis to ports on the east coast of England, notably Ipswich, with fresh produce especially tomatoes. With the introduction of containers in the early 1970s, the company established Geest North Sea Line which was to serve Hull and Tilbury in addition to Ipswich. This Line was taken over by Samskip in 2005. The **Geeststrom** was sold in 1976 and was renamed **Caravelle**. Three years later she was acquired by Cebo and converted to a cement carrier with tanks fitted in her hold. She entered service delivering Cebo's products from Delfzijl to ports such as Great Yarmouth, Aberdeen and Peterhead for use in drilling rigs. She is seen leaving Immingham on 9 April 2004. In early 2005 she was sold to owners in Ghana. Her tanks were removed by Orangewerf at Amsterdam and placed in the **Noblesse C**. She was then towed to Las Palmas with an ultimate destination named as Banjul. She was reported as still in service in 2014 but her last known movement was at Jeddah in 2009.

(Dominic McCall)

The Gebr. Buijs shipyard in Krimpen aan den IJssel traces its history back to founder Jan Buijs in 1859. He had worked for van der Giessen. Brothers Cornelis and Arie, also previous workers at the van der Giessen yard took over in 1930. It remains an independent company building ships and ship sections. This coaster was launched at the yard on 9 November 1977 and delivered as *Edgerma* in January of the following year. Despite passing through the hands of several owners and even renaming to *Germa* in 1994, E P Shipping & Trading, of Spijkenisse, remained managers until 2000. In 1995 her original 12-cylinder Caterpillar engine of 850bhp was replaced by a slightly more powerful Caterpillar model giving 865bhp. In early 2007 she was overhauled at the Dockside shipyard in IJsselmonde and later in the year arrived at Ridderkerk to be handed over to owners in Suriname and renamed *Daya 1*. By December she had switched to the Comoros flag and this was changed to the flag of Guyana in the following year. By 2011 she seemed to have been abandoned on the Suriname river near Paramaribo. She was photographed at the Dockside shipyard on 21 July 2007.

(Koos Goudriaan)

The shipyard of van der Giessen de Noord in Krimpen aan den IJssel can trace its history back to 1820. It had a fine reputation for building ferries but was closed in October 2003. The *Hehaluz II*, seen at Eastham on 24 August 1979, was launched at the yard on 30 December 1969 and completed for German owner H Bastia in February 1970. She was originally named *Sally Isle* for a charter to Sealand and in 1974 her name was amended to *Sally* after purchase by Cypriot-flag operators. By 1978 she was trading regularly from the Israeli ports of Ashdod and Haifa to northern Europe and in 1979 she was bought by Israeli owners and renamed *Hehaluz II*. As such she operated a service between Ellesmere Port and Haifa. Sold and renamed *Zim Napoli II*

in 1983, she was chartered by Zim Israel and traded in the Mediterranean. Renamed *Sky Luck* and then *Vigour Maritime* in 1987, she was trading between China and Japan in the late 1980s. In June 1989 she arrived at Shanghai and in 1990 began service between Shanghai and Hong Kong as *Xiu Shan*. Sales within China saw her become *Cheng Gong 6* in 2000 and *Xin Hong Zhou 6* in 2006. Later in 2006 she hoisted the flag of Sierra Leone as *Old Lady*. By this time she had disappeared from movement reports and was deleted from registers in 2011 with her continued existence in doubt.

(David Gallichan)

One of the longest lasting shipbuilding yards at Capelle aan den IJssel was that of A Vuijk & Zonen. The New Waterway opened in 1872 and Adrianus Vuijk realised the possibilities for ship repair and building work that this would bring. The first vessel was built in 1875 and construction continued at various sites on the IJssel until 1980. In its later years, it tended to concentrate on specialised dredgers but in the early 1970s the yard built a series of feeder ships for Sea Containers Ltd. One of these was the *Tua*, launched on 18 August 1970 and delivered on 12 November. Chartered by Ellerman Lines, she became *City of Florence* in 1974. We see her in the River Mersey outward bound from Ellesmere Port on 3 September 1977. Her poor external condition and the fact that she is in ballast suggest that she was heading for a drydock. She became *Hustler Fal* in 1982 but never traded as such, being laid up in Manchester, and then *Confrigo 1* (1984), *Lorelei* (1989) and *Halcon del Mar* (1991). She continues to trade as such in 2015, generally trading between Georgetown (Guyana) and Nieuw Nickerie (Suriname).

(Laurie Schofield)

The IJsselwerf yard at Capelle aan den IJssel was one of the area's most productive in its heyday. Although it had been repairing ships for several years previously, the first newbuilding was not until 1951. The yard closed in 1999. In the 1970s, most of the production was oil rig supply ships with a few reefers and tankers. Conventional dry cargo ships were infrequent. The yard did, however, build two container ships for James Fisher, namely **Guernsey Fisher** and **Jersey Fisher**. Both were intended for bareboat charter to British Rail for its new service from Portsmouth to the Channel Islands. The **Jersey Fisher** was launched on 30 October 1971, completed on 15 February 1972 and made her maiden arrival in Jersey six days later. In October 1977 the service and charter were taken over by Commodore Shipping and she was renamed **Commodore Challenger**. Returned to her owners on 1 October 1983, she reverted to **Jersey Fisher** until bareboat chartered in June 1984 to J & A Gardner by whom she was renamed **Loch Awe**. Returned on 5 January 1991, she was sold to Portuguese owners and renamed **TMP Aquarius**. Subsequent sales saw her become **Amina Hamen** (2001), **Al Tayeb** (2003) and **Tala 1** (2006). She was recycled at Aliaga in February 2010.

(David Gallichan)

In the mid-1960s James Sherwood, a retired United States naval officer, saw the imminent demand for containers and in 1965 established Sea Containers Ltd as a container leasing business. The company also built ships to carry the containers, its first notable venture being the Hustler class from 1969 onwards, eight of which were taken on long term bareboat charter by Ellerman Lines. In 1970 one of the shipbuilders - Zaanlandsche Scheepsbouw Maatschappij N. V., Zaandam, was taken over by T. van Duijvendijks Scheepswerfen N. V., Lekkekerk. Subsequently some of the Zaanlandsche contracts were sub-contracted to Lekkekerk and given "Z" numbers. However, in 1972, it was decided that the Zaanlandsche yard would close, due to financial problems. The **City of Oporto** was launched at the Zaanlandsche yard in April 1970 and delivered as **Tormes** during June. She traded as **City of Oporto** between 1974 and 1980 and was then sold and renamed **Eco Guadiana**. She was laid up after arrival at Lisbon on 20 October 1983. She was still there four years later but then disappeared from reports. She is understood to have been renamed **Dina** in 1989 and indeed to be still trading but there are no details available. We see her at Eastham on 13 September 1977.

(David Gallichan)

The **Pergo** was launched at the van Goor shipyard in Monnickendam on 17 March 1976 and delivered on 25 May to G de Vries & Zoon, of Zaandvoort. She was involved in two serious incidents during her career, both off the east coast of the UK. On 13 January 1984, she was abandoned by her crew in very heavy weather when on passage from Landskrona to Montrose. Although without crew, she continued her voyage westwards and eventually grounded near Dunbar. Her master, the owner's son, had maintained headway so that the rescue could be effected. She was towed off and taken to Leith for repair, eventually returning to service on 10 February. In 1987 a sale within the Netherlands saw her renamed **Fivel**. In February 1995 she was laid up at Delfzijl and at the end of the year was bought by Captain Mike Clayton who renamed her **Rema** after his son Ren and daughter Emma. On 24 April 1998 she was about twenty miles east of Whitby on passage from Berwick-on-Tweed to Terneuzen with a cargo of stone when she sank so quickly that Captain Clayton was unable to finish his Mayday message. All five crew lost their lives including Captain Clayton and his brother. The reason for the sinking was never discovered although there was much speculation that she may have hit a container lost from a vessel two weeks previously and possibly floating beneath the surface. She was photographed in the River Ouse on 21 August 1979.

(David Gallichan)

The **Lenie** was launched at the van Goor shipyard in Monnickendam on 20 December 1978 and was delivered to owner Captain Rense Haan, of Groningen, on 17 March 1979. She had just completed her maiden voyage to Goole when photographed on 23 March. In July 1979 she was in collision with a vehicle carrier in thick fog in the River Humber and after completion of emergency repairs she sailed to Harlingen for permanent repairs that lasted six weeks. Despite passing through the hands of several owners until 1999 she was renamed only once, becoming **Willem** between 25 November 1995 and 26 September 1997. In 1999 she was acquired by Danish owners and renamed **Dan Server** on 29 April. She retained this name after being bought by Caribbean owners in 2007. Some six years later she was abandoned at Colon and remains there between other abandoned vessels and now half submerged. Willem van Goor, a shipbuilder based in Kampen, bought the aan de Haven shipyard at Monnickendam in 1922. This yard had been owned by the Kater family since the seventeenth century. Until its closure in 1982, the yard produced many barges for inland waterways in addition to coasters.

(Laurie Schofield)

We have already noted that the distinction between a barge and a coaster can be minimal. The geography of the Friesland area of the northern Netherlands made it inevitable that Dutch barge owners would seek to push their trading limits towards Germany and even beyond. By the 1960s, vessels were being built specially for trading in this area and were known as Hamburgvaarders or Denemarkenvaarders. Construction continued well into the 1970s. Van Goor's shipyard was ideal for the construction of such vessels and in 1972 delivered the *Trinitas* to an owner in Amsterdam. She worked as a Denemarkenvaarder for four years and then started to trade as a conventional coaster. In September 1977 she was sold to Hendrik Steenstra, of Kampen, and was renamed *Douwe S*, becoming *Thalassa* in mid-February 1981 when acquired by Geert Switynk, also of Kampen. She became *Andries* two years when

bought by Hette de Weerd, of Harlingen. She left Harlingen on 5 March 2001 with destination unknown but later in the year she was reported to have been renamed *Metraton* after purchase by Belgian owner Kapitein Samuel de Gadenne for trading on inland waterways. Sold in December of that same year, she reverted *Andries*. Her new owner was Lysiane Burdin, of Dijon. In very thick fog on the evening of 27 November 2002, she collided with a jetty at Haaften on the River Waal. So thick was the fog that a tug attempting a rescue had difficulty in seeing the coaster and it was not until the following morning that the *Andries* could be towed to a safe refuge. We see her on the Canal du Rhône in southern France on 21 August 2010.

(Annemarie van Oers)

This vessel was launched at the Peters shipyard in Kampen on 10 July 1975 and delivered as **Audrey Johanna** to Hendrik Buitenkamp, of Groningen, on 18 December. Management was entrusted to Wijnne & Barends until Poseidon took over in September 1981 after the ship had been sold to Jan Damhof Jr and Daniel Damhof, of Delfzijl, by whom she was renamed **Barok**. After arriving at Harlingen in July 1995, ownership was transferred to the local shipyard and in late September her name was modified to **Baron**. She was sold to Francois Kwekkeboom, of Veere, in January 1996 and renamed **Voyager**. With her owner seemingly in financial difficulties, she was laid up at Vlaardingen after arrival on 13 August 2003 and was eventually sold at public auction on 30 March 2005. She was towed to 's Gravendeel a few days later and was renamed **Lilly** in June 2005 but there seem to be no subsequent movement reports. We understand that she was renamed **Julia** by Syrian owners in November 2009 and then **Jalal** in October 2012. She was beached for recycling at Aliaga on Christmas Day 2013. It came as a huge shock when the Peters yard was declared bankrupt in early April 2014. There were reports that Bodewes had taken over the yard but as this book is being written in mid-2015, nothing has been confirmed. We see her as **Voyager** at Teignmouth in 1999.

(Bernard McCall)

The *Harma*, outward bound in the River Trent, was a smaller coaster than the *Voyager*. In fact the order had been given to the Amels shipyard in Makkum and had been allocated a yard number but Amels was unable to fulfil the contract within the specified time and the construction was handed to Peters. She was launched on 29 December 1978 and delivered on 12 April 1979. In mid-February 2000 she was sold to Troon-based Taylor & Taylor to work in the Scottish timber trade. She continued in this trade after being bought by Coast Lines Shipping Ltd in 2007. Four years later, she was sold to a Dutch broker and was laid up at 's Gravendeel from 12 April 2011. In summer 2012 she was sold to owners in Miami and was reactivated at the Dockside shipyard in IJsselmonde. Retaining the name *Red Baroness* but now flying the flag of Bolivia, she left Rotterdam on 11 September 2012. Her transatlantic voyage was longer than anticipated. She docked at Las Palmas because of an overheating engine. There she was detained for over a month after port state control inspectors found numerous deficiencies. This could have been avoided. The overheating was caused by mussels in the coolers - a consequence of working near fish farms in Scotland. The coolers could have been cleaned at anchor simply by rodding. After arrival in Miami, she traded with relief supplies to Haiti.

(David Gallichan)

We see the *Dependent* in the River Ouse on 9 November 1978. She was launched at the Peters shipyard on 4 May 1977 and delivered to Dutch owners on 9 September. She was renamed *Anne* after a sale within the Netherlands in early 1982 and in the following year her original 8-cylinder Brons engine of 750bhp was replaced by a 12-cylinder Mitsubishi of 1001bhp. On 9 November 1985 she grounded on Scar Rocks just south of Hartlepool when approaching that port at the end of a voyage from Rotterdam and was later taken to Sunderland for inspection and repair. A further sale within the Netherlands saw her become *Dina Jacoba* in late 1987. On 3 September 2001 when near the Italian port of Olbia she was afflicted by machinery damage. Initially towed to Olbia, she was then towed to Piraeus for repairs on 17 September and resumed trade on 17 October. She had only just been acquired by Greek owners and renamed *Anemos* when the incident occurred. Later sales saw her become *Costis A* in November 2002 and *Svetla* in July 2004. She was reported at Illichevsk on 9 April 2005 and then disappeared from movement reports. However, she continued to trade mainly to Black Sea ports and was last reported to be heading south in the Red Sea in late June 2013 when on passage from Port Said to Yemen.

(Laurie Schofield)

The **Midsland** was launched on 29 June 1978 at the Amels "Friesland" shipyard in Lemmer. She was delivered on 15 September to van Nievelt, Goudriaan & Co for operation by that company's Scheepvaart- en Steenkolen (Shipping & Coal) subsidiary. She was dedicated to the company's Macvan container service between Rotterdam and Leith. We see her at Leith in October 1985. Sold to Cypriot flag operators in December 1987 she was renamed **Lady Aalke** and worked from Rotterdam and Antwerp to Portugal but in October 1988 she was sold to Piraeus-based Pelias Shipping Co Ltd, an enthusiast of good quality secondhand container ships from northern Europe. She linked Piraeus to Ravenna and Ancona until taken on charter by the Mediterranean Shipping Company in October 1999 and renamed **MSC**
Bosphorus for trade between Piraeus and Thessalonika. She arrived at Eleusis for lay up on 30 March 2002 and then on 8 August 2003 she was renamed **Agios Arsenios** still in the ownership of Pelias Shipping and entered service between Thessalonika and Larimna. Laid up at the latter port from late May 2005, she was sold at the end of the year and from mid-January 2006 traded widely in the Mediterranean and Adriatic as **Bright Star 1**, In late December 2008, she was renamed **Star 1** and was last heard of trading between west Africa and the Cape Verde Islands and fitted with a mast amidships with two cranes.

(Alistair Paterson)

The Carebeka company was established in the Netherlands as a co-operative to work on behalf of many captain-owners and obtain the best possible terms for freight contracts. In 1956 the company bought its first vessel and gradually added to the owned fleet. This was not successful and ultimately brought about the end of Carebeka because owning ships was very different indeed from managing them commercially on behalf of others. The **Carebeka IX** was the final vessel to be owned. She was launched at the Friesland shipyard in Lemmer on 7 January 1977 and completed on 2 March. With Carebeka in great financial difficulties, the vessel was sold within the Netherlands and bareboat chartered to Wagenborg's as **Elsborg**. Sold in mid-November 1988, she became **Artemis** but reverted to **Elsborg** in 1994. In the following year she was acquired by British operators and placed under the management of Torbulk Ltd. Renamed **Swanland** in 1996 she was then fitted with a self-discharge system. Her end was tragic. After loading stone at Raynes Jetty for delivery to Cowes, she sank in heavy weather off the Lleyn peninsula in North Wales on 27 July 2011. Of her all-Russian crew of eight, only two survived. We see her at Boston (Lincs) on 7 April 2009.

(David Dixon)

We now move to the north-west of the Netherlands and look at two coasters built by Scheepswerf- en Reparatiebedrijf 'Harlingen' which closed in 2011 after a 55-year existence. The Schöning family had been shipowners in Haren/Ems since the mid-nineteenth century. In the early 1970s, Hermann Schöning of the family's third generation in shipping, established the Intersee shipping company and ordered three coasters from different yards in the Netherlands. These were the *Alandsee*, *Bottensee* and *Chiemsee* which was launched on 24 November 1973 and completed on 21 December. In 1982 she was bought by Finnish owners and renamed *Chiemsea*, this changing to *Lotta* three years later. Although passing through the hands of various owners, she retained this name until becoming *Jampi* in 2001. In late January 2003 she was renamed *Nordbulk* and arrived at Szczecin on 9 September 2003 to be laid up pending sale. This was effected in early summer 2004 and she moved to the Mediterranean and Black Sea where she traded as *Lucy Mar*. In mid-December 2004 she was renamed *Olympic A* and kept this name until 2012. She was then converted to a livestock carrier and, now owned in Beirut, was renamed *Shrouk Livestock* this changing to *Alrayan* in 2013. She was photographed at Southampton on 12 April 2002.

(Chris Bancroft)

The **Frisian Star**, passing Rozenburg on the New Waterway, was the last of three sisterships built by Scheepswerf- en Reparatiebedrijf "Harlingen" for a consortium of owners that included members of the Holwerda and van der Schoot families, with the building yard having a 40% share in this vessel. Launched on 24 April 1978, she was delivered on 26 May. It is clear at first glance that she differed from other coasters of her generation that were being built in the Netherlands, thanks to her unusual midships mast and two derricks. She arrived at Harlingen to be laid up in early July 1986, joining her two sisters that had arrived there previously. All three were offered for sale at auction in Delfzijl on 20 February 1987. By mid-1988 she had been sold to German owner Hermann Buss and was renamed **Thaliena**. In the following year she became **Capto** after purchase by Norwegian interests. In 1993, she moved to the flag of the Bahamas but in Russian ownership as **Laverna** and was arrested at Thessalonika on 5 October 1995. There she remained until early 2003 when she was sold and renamed **Alkman**. She immediately disappeared from movement reports and still failed to appear after being sold and renamed **Portland** in early 2006. On 26 May 2006 she sank when on passage from Santa Cruz de Tenerife to Las Palmas with 2200 tons of cement. Sadly two members of her crew of eleven were lost.

(David Gallichan)

With her two 5-ton derricks the **Atlantic Wave** was another coaster to differ from many other Dutch-built vessels of her era. She was launched at the Franeker shipyard of Ton Bodewes on 19 October 1977 and was delivered as *Pechudo* to a consortium comprising mainly the Wildeman family on 18 January 1978. Management was entrusted to Wagenborg. On 13 March 1983 she arrived at Delfzijl from Liverpool and was laid up to await sale. She was sold at auction in Delfzijl on 30 April, the buyers being a Rotterdam company who entrusted management to Wijnne & Barends and named the vessel *Udo*. In November 1984 she was acquired by Oost Atlantic Lijn and renamed **Atlantic Wave**. We

see her outward bound at Eastham. She became **Frihav** after acquisition by Cypriot-flag operators in 1995. On 13 December 1998 she was approaching the port of Brens (Cée) in Galicia to load a cargo of ferromanganese when she grounded at Punta Galera south of Corcubión. A tug failed to refloat her and she broke in two during a storm on 30 December. This is the first reference to the name Bodewes which is to feature prominently on future pages. The Franeker yard was established by Ton Bodewes on 1 August 1956 and closed in 1991 after his death.

(David Gallichan)

The **Celtic Voyager** was one of a series of coasters built in the Netherlands for Weston Shipping (see page 56). In fact she was the last one in the series and was launched in three sections at the Ton Bodewes shipyard. These were joined together when afloat and the ship was towed to Harlingen for completion as **Alannah Weston** on 13 May 1975. In 1984 she was sold to Charles M Willie (Shipping) Ltd and was renamed **Celtic Voyager** with registry at Cardiff. We see her in the Roath Basin in her home port in August 1987. A sale to Russian owners in 1997 resulted in no change of name and she remained under Willie control. She was laid up at Slikkerveer near Rotterdam on 27 September 2000 and was reported to have been sold to owners in Canada in the following year. She retained the same name but switched to the Panamanian flag. She was noted at Miami in early July 2002 but then disappeared from movement reports and there is no further information about her.

(Bernard McCall)

This vessel was to have an interesting history which began even before her launch. She was the second of a pair ordered by the Hull Gates Shipping Company. She was bought when under construction by Consolidated Gold Fields Ltd to be managed by Comben Longstaff. She was built by Kramer & Booy in Kootstertille but the builders had underestimated the cost of construction of these two ships and four earlier ships for Danish owners. As a consequence Kramer & Booy suffered bankruptcy in February 2005 and the liquidators assigned completion of the ships to the Amels shipyard at Makkum. The Kootstertille shipyard soon revived as Tille Scheepsbouw as we see on the next page. The yard became part of the Conoship consortium. The ship was launched as *Lancasterbrook* on 3 October 1975 and completed in the following month. We see her in the Botlek area of Rotterdam on 26 May 1980.

(Bernard McCall)

An early charter saw the ship and her sister *Londonbrook* taken on charter by North Africa Line for trade to Limassol, Ashdod and Haifa. To avoid problems with Arab nations who had a blacklist of ships with Israeli connections, both vessels were transferred to a newly-created company and were renamed, *Lancasterbrook* becoming *Chelseastream* in November 1976. She reverted to her original name in December 1979 on completion of the charter. In June 1990 she was sold to Greek operators and was renamed *Prime Vision*. She traded mainly between Limassol, Piraeus and Port Said. Sold to Maltese flag operators in 1993 and renamed *Adriatic Star*, her trading pattern altered so that she worked between Ravenna, Piraeus and Beirut. Later changes of name saw her become *Blue Eye* (1999), *Amina* (2002), *Blue Eye* again (2004), *Hibat Allah* (2005), *Laguna* (2008), *United* (2011) and finally *Agapito* (2014). The latter name was shortlived as she arrived at Aliaga for recycling on 10 May 2014. When photographed at Sharjah on 2 February 2004, she carried no port of registry and flew no flag.

(Roger Hurcombe)

Sylvia Cargo was founded in 1958 and after twenty years of slow growth a major expansion was planned in the late 1970s. Six new vessels were ordered from four different yards in the Conoship group. With poor freight rates in the early 1980s, Sylvia Cargo was finding it difficult to service the debts on its six new ships and the company went out of business in March 1985 with its ships being sold to other Dutch companies. The **Sylvia Gamma**, seen leaving Swansea for Tonnay Charente on 21 July 1982, was the second of the three to have been built at the Tille shipyard in Kootstertille. She was launched on 14 December 1977 and delivered on 28 January 1978. After the collapse of the company she arrived at Rotterdam on 3 April 1985 and was soon sold to a company associated with Heinrich Hanno, of Rotterdam, as indeed were three other Sylvia vessels. She was renamed **Vijverhof** and then **Caspic** in 1994. Sold to Syrian owners in 2001, she was handed over at Antwerp and renamed **Ghewa B** on 8 November. She departed for Lattakia on the next day. Ten years later she became **Amal** and arrived for recycling at Aliaga in late March 2012. The Tille shipyard, which took over the Kramer & Booy yard in 1976, was itself declared bankrupt in 2003.

(Bernard McCall)

In the 1960s Associated British Foods Ltd (ABF), founded by the Canadian Garfield Weston and comprising other companies involved in food production and marketing, sought to safeguard its supply and distribution network by establishing its own shipping company. This was Weston Shipping and after buying two secondhand coasters it approached Conoship, the marketing arm of several Dutch shipyards, to build nine vessels. The *Jana Weston* was the first to be delivered. We see her passing Meredyke on 28 August 1977. A product of the Wartena shipyard of G Bijlsma & Zoon, she was launched on 23 September 1971 and completed on 10 November. By the early 1980s, trading conditions had changed considerably. Not only had freight rates fallen but by 1984 domestic wheat production in the UK had doubled since 1970. In 1984, the *Jana Weston* was sold to British buyers and was renamed *Borelly*. She has retained this name and was trading as such in the Gulf of Mexico and Panama Canal area during 2015. She has been fitted with a small wheelhouse above her bridge to allow better vision over deck cargoes.

(David Gallichan)

The **Noordland**, about to pass beneath the Humber Bridge, was launched at the Bijlsma shipyard in Wartena on 9 September 1977 and delivered on 14 October to a company based in Lemmer. Following several changes of ownership within the Netherlands over the next decade she became **Stepenitz** when bought by German operators in 1989. Later sales within Germany saw her become **Mona Lisa** (1999), **Monika** (2004), **Christa Kerstin** (2008) and then **Idil** in 2012 after purchase by a British company but flying the flag of Dominica. She was trading in the Dubai area in mid-2015. The Bijlsma family was building barges in Wartena in the late 18th century. Thanks to its membership of the Conoship group, orders were plentiful in the 1960s and 1970s. As the demand for larger ships increased, the Wartena site became problematic because of restricted waterway access to the IJsselmeer. So in 1995, Bijlsma bought the Friesland yard in Lemmer from Cees Amels. In 2003/4, both yards were declared bankrupt and were taken over by the VeKa Group. With Arend Bijlsma as a director of the new company at Lemmer and another family member, Tjeerd Wiebe Bijlsma, keen to revive shipbuilding at Wartena though on a smaller scale, the company prospers once again.

(David Gallichan)

In the late 19th century, the Holwerda family was involved in transporting turf by barge. Over the next half century, the family steadily acquired more and bigger vessels. Tonnage lost during World War 2 was replaced in the 1950s and two decades later the company wished to take advantage of the new post-1969 regulations with some vessels built to the 60 metre limit. The order for five new ships was given to the Barkmeijer shipyard in Stroobos and three further ships of the distinctive design were built for other owners. The goalpost mainmast and tripod foremast, each with a 5-ton derrick, were obvious features and the ice classification enabled trade to Alaska. The **Elisabeth Holwerda**, seen at Eastham on 25 February 1981, was launched on 7 November 1975 and completed on 12 December. She remains in service in 2015 and it is worth noting that although she switched to the Cypriot flag in 1987 and then to that of Antigua & Barbuda in 2004, she has always remained in Dutch ownership. She became **Elina B** in 1987 and then **Elina** (1991), **Blue Moon** (1997) and **Layla** (2004). The Barkmeijer yard at Stroobos is still very busy.

(David Gallichan)

The **Margarita Weston** was the smallest of the nine coasters ordered by Weston Shipping and she was intended for trade to the mill at Rochford in Essex. She was launched at the Barkmeijer shipyard in Vierverlaten on the outskirts of Groningen on 27 February 1975. The Barkmeijer family had owned several shipyards in the Groningen area, that at Vierverlaten being taken over in 1930 and closing in 1976. The **Margarita Weston** was completed on 26 March and proved to be one of the yard's last vessels. She was sold to Canadian owners in 1983 and her name was changed to simply **Margarita** and this was amended to **Margarita IV** following a sale in 1996. Becoming **Apkito 1** in

1997, she had long disappeared from movement reports. Later changes of name saw her become **Flora I** (1999), **Faith** (2000) and finally **Capt Hermon H** in 2005. Flying the flag of Nicaragua, she was beached at Puerto Cabello in Venezuela in December of that year. A new crew had been taken on board the previous month but by mid-July 2007 they were complaining of non-payment since they had joined the ship which was declared a constructive total loss the following year. On 21 August 1976 she was on the River Ouse and heading for Selby.

(David Gallichan)

The shipyard of Gebr. Sander was established at Delfzijl in 1927. In 1980 it merged with the Niestern shipyard to become Niestern Sander and celebrated its centenary in May 2001. At the same time in recognition of its contribution to Dutch shipbuilding, it was granted the prefix "Royal" and became Royal Niestern Sander. On 6 October 1979, this coaster was launched and was delivered as **Globe** to Beck's Scheepvaartkantoor on 1 November. She served her owner well until the summer of 1993 when she was bought by Dundalk Shipping Co Ltd and renamed **Rockfleet**. Seven years later she was acquired by Vincent Nolan, of Dublin, and was renamed **Clonlee**. We see her at Sharpness thus named on 6 January 2003. In mid-2003 she was renamed **Globia** after coming under the control of the RMS Group in Lübeck. She continued at work in northern Europe in mid-2015.

(Cedric Catt)

Launched at the Sander shipyard on 28 February 1976, the **Gallic Wave** was one of a pair of ships ordered by Gallic Shipping in the mid-1970s. Although of similar appearance and tonnages, they were of different dimensions and so were not sisterships. Sold to an associated company in 1983 she was renamed **All State** and remained on time charter to Jebsens. Gearless when built, she had been fitted with a mast and two derricks by the late 1980s but this detail did not appear in registers. From her entry into service, she had been managed by companies within the Denholm Group. She arrived at Rotterdam for repairs on 23 April 1989 and departed for Kinsale on 3 May under the new name of **Glentrool**. By the end of that year she had been sold to Maltese-flag operators and had been renamed **Cova da Iria**. She later became **Valda Ir** (1992), **Chahaya Sejati** (1994) and finally, under North Korean ownership, **Misan** (1999). She was broken up in China in spring 2003. We see her outward bound in the River Mersey at Eastham on 4 June 1977.

(David Gallichan)

We now look at ships built along the waterway known as the Winschoterdiep. This vessel was launched at the van Diepen shipyard in Waterhuizen on 27 August 1976 and delivered as **Mishnish** to J & J Denholm on 29 September. In 1987 she joined the fleet of Georgios Roussos and was transferred to the Cypriot flag as **G Roussos II**. Eight years later she was acquired by Latvian interests and became the Maltese-flagged **Maxim**. We see her arriving at Cardiff under this name on 18 August 1996. The next sale, in September 2001, saw her become **Jojo A** under the Tongan flag but she transferred to the flag of Georgia in 2004. On the evening of 6 January 2008, when on passage from Diliskilesi to Tartous with a cargo of china clay, she hit rocks on the Datça peninsula on the Turkish coast and began to settle in the water two days later. She was eventually declared a constructive total loss.

(Nigel Jones)

Dutch shipyards successfully tendered to build a succession of coasters for British owners, no doubt through the persuasion of Conoship. The Dutch yards had gained experience in building vessels within the limits of the new rules introduced in 1969 and the British owners were keen to take advantage of Dutch expertise. Turnbull Scott was expanding its fleet at this time and ordered two vessels of 1598grt. The **Baxtergate** was launched at the Westerbroek yard of E J Smit & Zoon on 7 November 1975 and completed on 22 January 1976. Four years later she entered the fleet of Belfast-based John Kelly Ltd when that company was seeking to replace older vessels and she was renamed **Ballykern**. After a further ten years, she was bought by yet another British company, namely Powell Duffryn. With management going to its Stephenson Clarke subsidiary, she was renamed **Lancing** and is seen here as such in Cawsand Bay on 16 August 1997. Sold later in 1997 to operators in the eastern Mediterranean, she was renamed **Al Farook** at Shoreham on 24 August and sailed to Antwerp where she loaded for Port Said and Alexandria. Having been renamed **Haroun** (2001) and **Marmara M** (2002), she disappeared from movement reports after leaving Iskendrun for Tartous on 11 March 2005. She is understood to have been delivered for recycling at Aliaga in April 2013.

(Nigel Jones)

The *Slano* is a rather different vessel from the van Diepen shipyard. Her two sturdy masts to each of which is attached a substantial derrick show her to be a heavy-lift ship. In fact each derrick is capable of lifting 180 tons. Launched on 30 June 1978 she was delivered to Rotterdam-based owners as *Valkenier* on 23 August. Nine years later she entered the fleet of Atlantska Plovidba in Dubrovnik, a port then in Yugoslavia but later to be Croatia. She was renamed *Slano* and retained this name until bought by Naples-based Medlift in January 2002. In March 2003 she became *Nikhil* under the flag of Panama. She was loading a transformer at Derince on 22 July 2004 when she capsized and sank, sadly a member of her crew losing his life. She is seen in the Houston ship channel on 15 August 1996. The van Diepen shipyard was opened in 1878 and remained in family ownership until its closure in 2002. Five years later, the yard reopened as Groningen Shipyard and has quickly become a prominent builder of coasters and inland waterway craft.

(Nigel Jones)

Next to the van Diepen yard was that of J Pattje, established in 1778 and closed in 2003. Revived by the Groningen Scheepsbouw Combinatie in 2009, the latter company also failed but the yard has now become part of Groningen Shipyard. It was on 8 November 1977 that the **Helgezee** was launched at the shipyard of J Pattje. She was delivered to owners in Delfzijl as **Silvia** on 13 January 1978. Renamed **Helgezee** in 1983, this was changed to **Helge** after sale to German owners two years later. She took a third girl's name when she changed hands within Germany in 1989 and became **Sigrid**. She remained trading in northern Europe after being sold and renamed **Golf Star**

in autumn 1993. On 15 October 1994 she had to be towed to Swansea after suffering engine failure off St David's Head. Just over a year later she again suffered engine failure when on passage from Arklow to Rostock with a cargo of stone. On this occasion she grounded on the island of Scalpay. Her master declined help from local fishing boats and by the time that the tug **Anglian Earl** arrived from Lowestoft, there was no hope of salvage. Her crew was taken off by helicopter and the vessel was abandoned. Parts are still visible. We see her approaching Cardiff on 1 November 1986 with timber from Archangel.

(Bernard McCall)

Otto Danielsen established his own shipbroking company in Copenhagen on 1 April 1944. He wanted to be ready to assist in the rebuilding of the Danish merchant fleet once World War 2 had ended. He proved to be hugely successful and handled all sales for major Danish companies such as DFDS, Lauritzen and East Asiatic. In 1958 he became exclusive broker for the newly-established building yard of Ørskovs Staalskibsværft in Frederikshavn. The yard's first sixteen ships were modern trawlers that proved difficult to sell to Danish fishermen who preferred old wooden vessels. Danielsen and some friends and fellow investors bought the first four trawlers. He also bought the yard's first cargo vessel, built in 1962. His own owning account had started ten years previously when he bought one of two ships in a deal which he had brokered with the Nobiskrug shipyard in Rendsburg. In future years, however, he was always keen to use Dutch yards for newbuildings and the *Otto Danielsen* was the first of a series built at various yards in the Netherlands. She was launched at the Westerbroek yard of E J Smit & Zonen on 6 December 1974 and delivered as *Egyptian* on 28 February 1975. On completion of the time charter to Ellerman, she became *Otto Danielsen* in November 1976. She was sold to owners in Indonesia in 1990 and was renamed *Loka*, becoming *Bahari 2* in 2005. She is thought to be still trading. We see her at Barry discharging potatoes from Egypt on 25 January 1989.

(Bernard McCall)

Launched at the same Westerbroek yard on 4 February 1977, this vessel was a sistership of the **Otto Danielsen** and was delivered to her owners as **Mariane Danielsen** on 15 April. On 20 January 1989 she ran aground off the Icelandic port of Grindavik as she left that port for Akureyi. Sold to a local owner during April, she was towed off by a tug from Reykjavik and, after temporary repairs, was towed to Gdynia for permanent repairs. Later in the year she was sold unrepaired to Eide Shipping and on 10 October left Gdynia on a barge towed by the tug **Stril Power**, heading for Helsingør. Her travels were not yet over as she left Helsingør on 27 October, towed by the tug **Mega**

Mammut to Stavanger. By August 1990 she had been repaired and was renamed **Maylin** by Cypriot flag operators. She was soon trading out of Havana and it is thought that the Cuban government may have been involved in the purchase. She was renamed **Lupus** following a sale in 2009 and is understood to have been broken up in 2012. We see her at Havana on 22 March 1999. The yard at Westerbroek closed in 1978 but the company name was revived in 1991 by a member of the Smit family leading a ship design company connected to other yards.

(Nigel Jones)

The shipyard of Ferus Smit at Foxhol was opened in 1907 as J Smit en Zoon. It became Scheepswerf Ferus Smit v/h J Smit en Zoon in the 1950s and in 1989 it took over the yard of Jac Bodewes at nearby Hoogezand. Having adopted a naming scheme using the suffix "ity", F T Everard was sometimes compelled to be inventive and flexible in creating names. It may seem that **Grit** pushed the boundary of flexibilty but this vessel was the seventh to have carried the name - and was one of four thus named to have been lost. This coaster was one of four built in the Netherlands in the mid-1970s and the second of a pair built at the Ferus Smit yard in Foxhol. She was launched on 11 March 1976 and completed on 14 April. She had a relatively short career. On 25 January 1988, when nearing the end of a voyage from Rotterdam to Gunness, she sank in the Humber estuary after colliding with a dredger that was at anchor. Over two months later, she was raised in two sections both of which were taken to New Holland for breaking up. She was photographed as she left Teignmouth on 15 April 1984.

(Bernard McCall)

It was the building of the **Marco** that helped to revive the fortunes of the Ferus Smit shipyard. She was launched on 14 June 1977 and delivered to Captain Christof Leijten, of Zwijndrecht, on 22 August. Sold in 1984 she was renamed **Stern** and then became **Stera** after a further sale in 1992. She was involved in a serious incident in the Danish port of Aabenraa in December 1994. She suffered a fire in her galley. An investigation discovered that her master was sailing with three unqualified crew members. He himself had driven the ship for sixty hours without a break and the fire broke out after he had fallen asleep with a pan unattended in the galley. The fire was discovered before extensive damage occurred. Sold to a Dutch owner in 1997, the ship was to be renamed **Omega V** but the prospective owner suffered bankruptcy before the sale was completed. She was bought by Polish owners and renamed **Laila** on 12 March 1998. She returned to Dutch ownership in 2003 and, now named **Orion**, became an inland waterways vessel. We see her at IJmuiden on 30 September 2013 with part of the huge Tata (formerly Hoogovens) steel works in the background.

(Richard Potter)

The history of the *Torridge*, seen at Eastham on 20 August 1981, is certainly one of the more unusual ones in this book. She was ordered by Johannes Bos, of Loga/Hamburg, and launched at the Bodewes yard in Martenshoek as *Mia Bos* on 28 April 1970. She was immediately chartered out and was delivered on 29 June as *Dynacontainer I*. Johannes Bos had little background in shipping but in 1950 had taken over the fleet of his late father-in-law Gerd de Buhr. By the end of 1971 he had a fleet of 22 ships but was finding it impossible to service the mortgages. The banks involved distributed the ships to three different companies and this vessel, now named *Mia* with the charter ended, was one of ten to come into the Peter Döhle fleet. On 27 October 1976 she came into the British ownership of J E Hyde & Co and was renamed *Torridge*. By now, it was becoming increasingly common for

ships to have masts and derricks removed but a sale to Norwegian owners in 1983 saw the opposite happen to this ship. Renamed *Stensig*, she was fitted with two 30-ton derricks each supported by substantial goalpost masts and, on charter to Sloman Neptun, began a liner service linking Bremen and Bremerhaven to Norwegian ports. This continued after she was renamed *Perco Lifter* in 1991 and *Scan Lifter* in 1992. On 6 January 1993 she suffered an engine blackout when on passage from Bremen to Bergen and Ålesund. She grounded in Fensfjord and broke in two on 20 January. Bodewes Scheepswerven v/h G & H Bodewes is the oldest Bodewes shipyard. It opened under this name in 1912 but had already traded as G & H Bodewes for 200 years. The yard remains open as Royal Bodewes.

(David Gallichan)

The early history of the **Tropic** tends to mirror that of the **Torridge**. Also ordered by Johannes Bos, she followed the **Torridge** and was launched as **Dorothee Bos** but entered service as **Dynacontainer IV** in December 1970. When the Bos fleet was split in late 1971, she was one of eight taken into Hans Beilken's Mare Schiffahrtskontor. Her list of names over the next four years indicates some of the charterers. These names were **Tor Timber** (1971), **Dynacontainer IV** (1972), **Tropic** (1972), **Bell Chieftain** (1974) and **Tropic** (1975). On 10 September 1982 she left northern Europe when she departed Bremerhaven at the start of a voyage to Miami where she was renamed **Hybur Tropic**. Apart from the summer of 1988 when she returned to northern

Europe, she remained in the Caribbean and had several changes of identity which saw her become **Tropic** (1984), **Mer Star** (1988), **Carib Star** (1991) **Ann Mary** (1992), **Irma** (1993), **Allegro Sea** (1994), **Gulf Viking** (1996), **Dynacontainer I** and finally **Castor** (both in 1998). In 1999 the **Castor** was seized by U.S. Customs agents after being stopped by the Coast Guard carrying 10,127 pounds of cocaine. The captain and crew were arrested and the ship seized. The ship was sunk off Delray Beach, Florida, on 14 December 2001 as part of the Artificial Reef Programme of Palm Beach County. She was photographed outward bound at Eastham on 11 August 1978.

(Laurie Schofield)

Various members of the Bodewes family established shipyards in different parts of the Netherlands and this has caused some confusion. The **Procyon**, approaching the locks at Eastham on 23 October 1982, was launched at the Bodewes Gruno shipyard in Foxhol on 24 June 1977 and delivered to Schiedam-based owners on 3 September. In 1980 she was lengthened by seven metres at the Welgelegen shipyard in Harlingen. Four years later she entered the fleet of Arklow Shipping as **Arklow Valley** and in late 1991 she was renamed **Rockpoint** following bareboat charter to Dundalk Shipowners

Ltd. Five years later she joined the James Fisher fleet as **Solway Fisher**. The next sale saw her move to Latvian ownership when she became **Solvita** in 2001. After being laid up at Diliskelesi for several months, she arrived at Aliaga for recycling in late October 2012. The Bodewes Gruno yard was previously known as Bodewes Scheepswerf Volharding although the two yards had originally had separate sites. Bodewes Scheepswerf Volharding, founded in 1919, was taken over by the De Hoop shipyard in 2007.

(David Gallichan)

In the mid-1970s, F T Everard ordered six handy-sized coasters suitable for upriver trading. Four were built in the Netherlands to a Conoship design, two at the Ferus Smit yard and two at the Bijlholt shipyard in Foxhol. The *City* was the second of the pair from Bijlholt and was launched on 27 January 1976 with delivery during March. She served the Everard company well for almost two decades and was sold in mid-1995, being renamed *Bay Fisher*. That proved to be brief as in the following year she was sold to Norwegian owners. She left Goole on 10 July and was next reported as *Alrita* on 8 August. Some sources suggest that she had been briefly renamed *Arnhild* but she seems not to have traded under this name. Again some sources claim that she was fitted as a self-discharge vessel in 1994 but in fact the upgrading took place in 1996. We see her near Haugesund on 6 May 2004. The Bijlholt yard can trace its history back to 1763. It was taken over by Damen in 1984.

(David Dodds)

The image on the front cover provides evidence that the Dutch were not averse to painting their new vessels in dramatic colours. The **Tromp**, seen at Eastham on 22 September 1979, is a further example. She was launched at the Bijlholt shipyard in Foxhol on 18 May 1979 and delivered to Rotterdam-based J Vermaas on 4 July. A brief period of lay-up following the bankruptcy of her owner in January 1982 was followed by a sale to other Dutch owners without change of name. In early April 1984, she entered the fleet of Arklow Shipping as **Arklow Glen** and retained this name until acquired by Norwegian owners in 1994. A sale to owners in the Faroe Islands saw her become **Havfrakt** in February 2006. On 24 October 2010 she grounded at Gisundet when approaching Finnsnes with a cargo of fishmeal. Refloated with assistance, she was taken to Finnsnes where only a small leak in a ballast tank was found. She remains busy in Scandinavian waters.

(David Gallichan)

Another shipyard at Foxhol on the Winschoterdiep was that of Gebr. Suurmeijer, also known as the De Vooruitgang shipyard. Launched there on 5 August 1977 was the **Marion Bosma** and she was delivered to Bosma Shipping during the following month. She was managed by Oost Atlantic Lijn and this company bought her in June 1978, renaming her **Atlantic Horizon**. She became **Baltic Horizon** after purchase by Latvian owners in late December 1994. She left northern Europe for the Mediterranean after being sold to Syrian owners and renamed **Haje Azizeh** in September 2001.

Later sales saw her become **Amitie** in December 2005 and **Editor** in March 2008. We see her thus named as she navigates through the Bosphorus on 5 June 2009. In early 2010, Romanian buyers renamed her **Omar M** and in May 2012 she was converted to a livestock carrier named **Barhom II** after acquisition by Lebanese buyers. The Suurmeijer yard was taken over by Bijlholt in 1980, the latter itself being taken over, as we have read on page 72, by Damen in 1984.

(Neil Burns)

The yard of Gebr. Coops at Hoogezand ceased shipbuilding in 1983, just over a century after its foundation. It then started to manufacture parts of ships such as hatch covers and gantry cranes under the title of Coops & Nieborg. The **Calypso**, seen at Par on 21 September 1986, was launched at the yard on 24 March 1977 and completed on 22 April. Her initial owner was Hendrik Koerts who entrusted management to Carebeka. She was laid up at Delfzijl on 12 October 1981 and sold by auction on 23 November 1982 to M Smits who intended to use her in the steel export trade from the Hoogovens steelworks at IJmuiden to UK ports. Immediately seen to be unsuitable for this work, she was sold again in December 1982. On 4 January 1997 she suffered engine failure while on passage from Liverpool to Germany with fertiliser. She was towed to Swansea and resumed her voyage on 16 January after the completion of repairs. A remarkable feature of her career is that apart from two short interludes she has retained her original name despite having several owners in the Netherlands and then in Norway and finally Greece. She was **Alice** between 27 May 2005 and 23 November 1996, and **Calypso I** between 22 April and September 2002. She did not trade under the latter name. Once in Greek ownership, she was fitted with a crane and she continues to trade in mid-2015. Her name is sometimes transliterated as **Kalypso**.

(Cedric Catt)

This book includes photographs of three of the coasters built in the Netherlands for Weston Shipping, a division of Associated British Foods. When these were being built, the Norwegian agent for Conoship, a Mr Fredrik Odfjell, was seeking financial support for the construction of six cargo vessels designed in Bergen. Associated British Foods provided the finance through its subsidiary G W Holdings Shipping Ltd and the ships were demise chartered for ten years to Frendo London Ltd, Mr Odfjell's British company. The ships were built at six different yards within the Conoship group, the **Frendo Faith** being built by Scheepswerf "Voorwaarts" in Hoogezand. All six were repossessed in 1976 as Frendo was unable to maintain charter payments and

this vessel was renamed **Louise Weston**. We see her leaving Swansea on 12 February 1977. Sold in 1982 she was renamed **Louise** and she passed to Austrian owners as **Patziel** later in the same year. Later sales saw her renamed **Clarisa** in 1997 and finally **Seafighter 1** in 2001. She suffered a serious fire off the Greek coast in late April 2002 and after being laid up at Eleusis she was delivered for recycling at Aliaga in September 2003. Scheepswerf Voorwaarts v/h E. J. Hijlkema was established by E. J. Hijlkema in 1935. After his death in 1961, it was continued by his sons but was closed following bankruptcy in 1983.

(Nigel Jones)

The **Swallow**, photographed on the Manchester Ship Canal on 26 May 1978, was launched at the Bodewes shipyard at Hoogezand on 31 October 1974 and, although completed on 13 December, did not run trials until 2 January 1975. She remains in service forty years later but has passed through the hands of various Dutch owners during that time. After seven years in service she was bought by Beck's Scheepvaartkantoor and was renamed **Proton**. Having served Beck's for seventeen years, she was bought by owners in Papendrecht and became **Scorpio**. In early 2001 a further sale saw her renamed **Sereen** and also in May of that year she was fitted with a new bow section by Santierul Naval at Braila. In September 2006 she was bought by owners in Werkendam and renamed **DC-Merwestone**. In August 2007 and again in October 2008, she suffered steering problems. On the first occasion she had to be towed to Harlingen and on the second, to Birkenhead. Even more seriously she had severe engine problems when leaving Klaipeda on 28 January 2010. Taken initially to Gdynia she was then towed to Bremerhaven for permanent repair, arriving on 1 March 2010, As already noted, she is still trading and was renamed **DC-Eems** in July 2015.

(Laurie Schofield)

The **Elvi Kull** was launched at the yard of Scheepswerf Hoogezand on 19 May 1979 and delivered to Dutch owners as *Carpe Diem* on 23 June. Soon after delivery she was renamed *Carpe Diem II* and was sold to Dutch owners in 1981 and renamed *Sambre*. Subsequent sales within the Netherlands saw her become *Meran* (1989), *Ideaal* (1990) and *Daan* (1996). In 2005, she was bought by a German owner and renamed *Elvi Kull* under the flag of Antigua & Barbuda. In 1994 her original 6-cylinder Brons engine of 750bhp was replaced by an 8-cylinder Caterpillar of 973bhp. Scheepswerf Hoogezand was founded in January 1941 by Jac. Bodewes. The yard closed in 1985 and the site was taken over by the Ferus Smit shipyard in 1989. We see the **Elvi Kull** as she heads west along the Kiel Canal on 22 July 2005 soon after entering service for her new owner.

(Dominic McCall)

When launched on 24 February 1978, the **Thalassa** received considerable publicity. Not only was she hailed as the first in a new generation of low air draught coasters but she was also to be the last vessel to be built at the Bodewes Bergum shipyard under that name. The yard was opened on 16 August 1955 and ceased independent operation after the delivery of the **Thalassa** to Albertus and Jan Oosterveen, of Dordrecht, on 1 April 1978. From that point onwards the yard worked in co-operation with the Damen Shipyards Group and was taken over by that group in 1981. A sale within the Netherlands saw her renamed **Frisiana** in late December 1979 and we see her as such as she is about to pass beneath the Humber Bridge on 7 August 1983. Later changes of identity saw her renamed **Frisian** (1989), **Vera** (1990), **Elisabeth G** (1995) and **Henk van Otterloo** (1997). In mid-2001 she was acquired by Panamanian-flag operators and, now named **Otterloo** left Bilbao for Curaçao on 14 August. Sold and renamed **Reina Sofia** in late 2003, she switched to the flag of Colombia in 2005 and is thought to be still in service.

(Bernard McCall)

Union Transport (London) Ltd was established in mid-August 1946. It was a shipbroking company and initially handled cargoes of sugar loaded at Silvertown on the River Thames and destined for Basel where they would be delivered to chocolate manufacturers. The business gradually expanded, ships were chartered for single voyages and then time chartered. In 1973, the company bought its first ship on the secondhand market and others followed. Three years later it was decided to buy four new vessels which would be built at two yards in the Netherlands. It was intended that these ships would be able to take cargoes of sugar direct from Silvertown on the River Thames to Basel in Switzerland. The *Union Jupiter*, photographed at Exmouth on 12 February 1989, was the first of the pair built at the van Rossum shipyard in Dreumel. She was completed in September 1977.

(Bernard McCall collection)

The van Rossum yard, situated just off the River Waal, was opened in 1930 and initially built small wooden vessels. It soon expanded and received orders for specialised vessels from countries throughout the world including Venezuela and Sierra Leone. The yard built 66 special copra barges for Indonesia. It also built many vessels for the inland waterways of Europe. The yard closed in 1988.

The *Union Jupiter* was sold and renamed *Prion* in 1989 and her original 16-cylinder General Motors engine was replaced with a 16-cylinder Cummins in 1990. On 20 March 1992 she arrived at Delfzijl from Colchester and was laid up along with her three sisterships. All were sold at auction during October and the *Prion* was renamed *Tern*. A sale to Russian operators saw her become *Multi Coaster* and after a further sale within Russia in 2008 she was renamed *Mius*. She was reported to be trading in the Sea of Azov in mid-2015. We see her as *Tern* inward bound in the River Trent in July 1995.

(John Mattison)